EDINBURGH AND THE BORDERS
·
In Verse

In the same series:

Oxford and Oxfordshire In Verse edited by Antonia Fraser
Cornwall In Verse edited by Peter Redgrove
East Anglia In Verse and Prose edited by Angus Wilson
London In Verse edited by Christopher Logue

General Editor: Emma Tennant

W.K. Ritchie

8. VIII. 87

EDINBURGH AND THE BORDERS

·

In Verse

·

edited and with an introduction by

ALLAN MASSIE

Secker & Warburg · London

First published in England 1983 by
Martin Secker & Warburg Limited
54 Poland Street, London W1V 3DF

British Library Cataloguing in Publication Data
Edinburgh and the borders in verse.
    1. English poetry   2. Scotland in literature
    I. Massie, Allan
    821'.008'0324134   PRI175

    ISBN 0-436-27348-9

Photoset in Great Britain by
Rowland Phototypesetting Ltd, Bury St Edmunds, Suffolk
and printed by St Edmundsbury Press
Bury St Edmunds, Suffolk.

for Alexander, Louis and Claudia

CONTENTS

ACKNOWLEDGEMENTS

Norman MacCaig: 'Crossing the Border' from *Rings on a Tree*, 'Edinburgh Courtyard in July' from *A Common Grace*, 'Drop-Out in Edinburgh' from *The World's Room*, 'Milne's Bar' from *The White Bird* and 'Double Life' from *Riding Lights* reprinted by permission of the author and The Hogarth Press Ltd.

Lewis Spence: 'The Firth', 'Colinton' and 'Craigentinnie' from *Collected Poems* reprinted by permission of Rhoda Spence.

Robert Garioch: 'Glawmrie', 'At Robert Fergusson's House', 'Embro to the Ploy', 'Cooling-Aff' and 'A Wee Local Scandal' from *The Complete Poetical Works of Robert Garioch* reprinted by permission of Macdonald Publishers, Edinburgh.

John Buchan: 'Fisher Jamie' reprinted by permission of The Rt Hon Lord Tweedsmuir.

Stewart Conn: 'End of Season, Drumelzier', 'New Town, Autumn' and 'Near Morebattle' reprinted by permission of the author. 'Choral Symphony' from *A Sense of Belonging: Six Scottish Poets of the Seventies* reprinted by permission of the author and Blackie & Son Ltd.

Hugh MacDiarmid: 'Dante on the Edinburgh People' and 'Old Wife in High Spirits' from *The Complete Poems of Hugh MacDiarmid 1920–1976* reprinted by permission of Mrs Valda Grieve and Martin Brian & O'Keeffe Ltd.

George Barker: 'Scottish Bards and an English Reviewer' from *The View from a Blind I* reprinted by permission of Faber & Faber Ltd.

Alan Bold: 'Edinburgh' reprinted by permission of the author.

Every effort has been made to discover the owners of copyright material reprinted. On receiving notification, any omissions that have occurred will be rectified.

ILLUSTRATIONS

All the illustrations in this book are reproduced by permission of Mary Evans Picture Library.

INTRODUCTION

To put together an anthology of verse representing Edinburgh and the Borders is a task that is both enviable and difficult. It is enviable because the editor will pass many happy hours exploring the rich vein of poetry written in these parts or occasioned by them; difficult because the choice is abundant and the criterion for selection endlessly discussable.

Edinburgh is a city, and the Borders are a region, of outstanding beauty. They are also steeped in history and legend, and this seemed to me to preclude my compiling an anthology of principally topographical or descriptive verse; yet the fact that this book belongs to a series which sets out to display different parts of Britain in verse meant that I have felt obliged to leave out much that I might have wished to include, whenever it did not appear to be anchored to a particular place.

Though it might seem that either Edinburgh or the Borders could separately have made for a more satisfyingly homogenous collection – a decision which would certainly have meant that I did not have to omit much that I would have liked to include – there is nevertheless good reason to take them together.

This reason is in the first place historical. Though other parts of Scotland may now make noisier claims to express the authentic character (whatever that is) of the country and nation, and though the Highlands may, on account of their spectacular beauty and sad Romantic past, have stamped themselves on the popular and commercial mind as the true image of Scotland, yet it remains the case that most of Scotland's history as an independent kingdom can be read in Lothian and the Borderlands.

John Buchan, who spent the happiest part of his youth on Tweedside, identified Dunbar, Burns, Scott and the Ballads as Scotland's 'main contributions to letters'. The Borders are one of the two regions richest in Ballads (the other is Aberdeenshire and the North-East). Dunbar lived much of his life in Edinburgh (though I have not found it possible to represent him here), while Walter Scott belonged to both Edinburgh and the Borders.

The Borders have inspired two sorts of verse. The Ballads are the best known of these of course, and the great Riding Ballads give the most vivid picture of the life of this kind of society that you can find outside Homer. But there is another sort of Ballad too, which tells of the supernatural and fairyland; I have included the best and most famous of these, *True Thomas*. It reminds one that the Eildon Hills (split in three, reputedly, by the wizard, Michael Scott) are associated with that richest of legends, the Matter of Britain itself; King Arthur is buried there, according to legend.

With the Union of the Crowns, the old warlike Border was gradually pacified; and when Walter Scott had revealed its beauties, especially in the verse epistles which precede each canto of *Marmion*, it spawned a quantity of pastoral verse. Not much of this – not even Wordsworth's three *Yarrow* poems – is of the highest quality, but the best has a quiet charm; it reveals the country lovingly. Has any stream ever been sung so often and so lovingly as Yarrow?

There is more variety in the Edinburgh verse. Some poets have responded to Scott's description of it as 'mine own Romantic town', and have sung of the public splendour of its situation and history; others have been more attracted to the roughness and frequent squalor of its low life. Only a few have written of its bourgeois and suburban charms. Trying to achieve some sort of balance which would represent the character of the city has not been easy.

Apart from Scott, there have been three supreme Edinburgh poets: that doomed youth of genius, Robert Fergusson, and in our own times Robert Garioch and Norman MacCaig. No one gives us the old eighteenth century city that tumbled down the Royal Mile from the Castle to Holyrood and swarmed hecticly in the pestiferous closes, more completely and with more brio than Fergusson; and I have chosen to represent him (and that city) by his masterpiece *Auld Reikie*. Garioch's tribute to Fergusson is as moving as anything in the book, and it shows his range of tone, but he is pre-eminently the poet of the little man, unimpressed by pretension and scornful of hypocrisy. *Embro to the Ploy* cocks a joyous snook at the city's cultural life. As for MacCaig, he is simply capable of saying more in less space than anyone else now writing. Together, Garioch and MacCaig delineate the character and nature of the city. I could have wished to include also the much-loved

Sydney Goodsir Smith, but he is a poet best read in bulk; his master-piece *Under the Eildon Tree* suffers too much from abridgement or selection for that to be desirable. To have included it would have required Fergusson to be severely pruned; undesirable from the point of view of balance, apart from other reasons.

I have not divided the book into two sections, and, like so many anthologists, I make the plea (probably a vain one) that the reader will gain from reading the poems in the order in which they appear. My intention has been to construct a mosaic of the regions, to help readers to look at them and to connect landscape and city with life as it has been lived and is lived today.

Allan Massie

SIR WALTER SCOTT

[1771–1832]

Introductory Poem

Breathes there the man, with soul so dead,
Who never to himself hath said,
'This is my own, my native land!'
Whose heart hath ne'er within him burned,
As home his footsteps he hath turned,
    From wandering on a foreign strand! –
If such there breathe, go, mark him well;
For him no minstrel raptures swell;
High though his titles, proud his name,
Boundless his wealth as wish can claim;
Despite those titles, power, and pelf,
The wretch, concentred all in self,
Living, shall forfeit fair renown,
And, doubly dying, shall go down
To the vile dust, from whence he sprung,
Unwept, unhonoured, and unsung.

O Caledonia! stern and wild,
Meet nurse for a poetic child!
Land of brown heath and shaggy wood,
Land of the mountain and the flood,
Land of my sires! what mortal hand
Can e'er untie the filial band,
That knits me to thy rugged strand!
Still, as I view each well-known scene,
Think what is now, and what has been,
Seems as, to me, of all bereft,
Sole friends thy woods and streams were left;
And thus I love them better still,
Even in extremity of ill.
By Yarrow's stream still let me stray,
Though none should guide my feeble way;

Still feel the breeze down Ettrick break,
Although it chill my withered cheek;
Still lay my head by Teviot stone,
Though there, forgotten and alone,
The Bard may draw his parting breath . . .

from 'The Lay of the Last Minstrel'

[b. 1910]

Crossing the Border

I sit with my back to the engine, watching
the landscape pouring away out of my eyes.
I think I know where I'm going and have
some choice in the matter.

I think, too, that this was a country
of bog-trotters, moss-troopers,
fired rucks and roof-trees in the black night – glinting
on tossed horns and red blades.
I think of lives
bubbling into the harsh grass.

What difference now?
I sit with my back to the future, watching
time pouring away into the past. I sit, being helplessly
lugged backwards
through the Debatable Lands of history, listening
to the execrations, the scattered cries, the
falling of roof-trees
in the lamentable dark.

WILLIAM DRUMMOND OF HAWTHORNDEN

[1585–1649]

Edinburgh

Install'd on hills, her head near starry bowres,
Shines Edinburgh, proud of protecting powers.
Justice defends her heart; Religion east
With temples, Mars with towers doth guard the west.
Fresh nymphs and Ceres serving wait upon her,
And Thetis' tributary doth her honour.
The sea doth Venice shake, Rome Tiber beats,
Whilst she but scorns her vassal water's threats.
For sceptres nowhere stands a town more fit,
Nor place where the world's queen may fairer sit.
But this thy praise is, above all, most brave,
No man did e'er defame thee but a slave.

A free translation from the Latin of Arthur Johnston

LEWIS SPENCE

[1874–1955]

The Firth

Yon auld claymore the Firth o' Forth,
Yon richt Ferrara o' the North,
Upon whase steel the broon sails scud,
Staining the blade like draps o' bluid,
Lies drawn betwixt the North and South,
A sword within the Lyon's mouth.
And in yon fell chafts shall it lie
Sae lang as there is Albanie,
Stapping the roar o' meikle jaws,
Point tae the hert and hilt to paws
O' yon auld rampant, girning baste
Wha o' cauld steel luves best the taste.

Like tae a watter on a wab
Woven wi' silks o' gowd and drab,
Scamander on a palace wall
Shone never mair majestical,
And like a castel sewn in soye
The turrets o' the Scottish Troy
Atowre that meikle moat rise up
Like weirds abune a witch's cup –
A wondrous ferlie frae the sea
Warth a hale warld o' poesie!

soye: silk   *ferlie*: marvel

WILLIAM HENRY OGILVIE
[1869–1964]

On a Roman Helmet
(Found at Newstead)

A helmet of the legion this,
  That long and deep hath lain,
Come back to taste the living kiss
  Of sun and wind again.
Ah! touch it with a reverent hand,
  For in its burnished dome
Lies here within this distant land
  The glory that was Rome!

The tides of sixteen hundred years
  Have flowed, and ebbed, and flowed,
And yet – I see the tossing spears
  Come up the Roman Road;
While, high above the trumpets pealed,
  The eagles lift and fall,
And, all unseen, the war-god's shield
  Floats, guardian, over all!

Who marched beneath this gilded helm?
  Who wore this casque a-shine?
A leader mighty in the realm?
  A soldier of the line?
The proud patrician takes his rest
  The spearman's bones beside,
And earth who knows their secret best
  Gives this of all their pride!

With sunlight on this golden crest
    Maybe some Roman guard,
Set free from duty, wandered west
    Through Memory's gates unbarred;
Or climbing Eildon cleft in three,
    Grown sick at heart for home,
Looked eastward to the grey North Sea
    That paved the way to Rome.

Or by the queen of Border streams
    That flowed his camp beneath
Long dallied with the dearer dreams
    Of love, as old as death,
And doffed his helm to dry lips' need,
    And dipped it in the tide,
And pledged in brimming wine of Tweed
    Some maid on Tiber-side.

Years pass; and Time keeps tally,
    And pride takes earth for tomb,
And down the Melrose valley
    Corn grows and roses bloom;
The red suns set, the red suns rise,
    The ploughs lift through the loam,
And in one earth-worn helmet lies
    The majesty of Rome.

SIR WALTER SCOTT
[1771–1832]

Melrose Abbey

If thou wouldst view fair Melrose aright,
Go visit it by the pale moonlight;
For the gay beams of lightsome day
Gild, but to flout, the ruins gray.
When the broken arches are black in night,
And each shafted oriel glimmers white;
When the cold night's uncertain shower
Streams on the ruined central tower;
When buttress and buttress, alternately,
Seem framed of ebon and ivory;
When silver edges the imagery,
And the scrolls that teach thee to live and die;
When distant Tweed is heard to rave,
And the owlet to hoot o'er the dead man's grave,
Then go – but go alone the while –
Then view St David's ruined pile;
And, home returning, soothly swear,
Was never scene so sad and fair . . .

'In calling back the sins of my youth I was surprised into confessing, what I might as well have kept to myself, that I had been guilty of sending persons a-bat-hunting to see the ruins of Melrose by midnight, which I never saw myself. The fact is rather curious, for as I often spent nights at Melrose (when I did not reside so near the place), it is singular that I had not seen it by moonlight on some chance occasion. However, it so happens that I never did, and must (unless I get cold going on purpose) be contented with supposing that these ruins look very like other Gothick buildings which I have seen by the wan light of the moon . . .'

Sir Walter Scott

Melrose Abbey

ANDREW LANG
[1844–1912]

Twilight on Tweed

Three crests against the saffron sky,
　Beyond the purple plain,
The kind remembered melody
　Of Tweed once more again.

Wan water from the Border hills,
　Dear voice from the old years,
Thy distant music lulls and stills,
　And moves to quiet tears.

Like a loved ghost thy fabled flood
　Fleets through the dusky land;
Where Scott, come home to die, has stood,
　My feet returning stand.

A mist of memory broods and floats,
　The Border waters flow,
The air is full of ballad notes,
　Borne out of long ago.

Old songs that sung themselves to me,
　Sweet through a boy's day-dream,
While trout below the blossom'd tree
　Plashed in the golden stream.

Twilight, and Tweed, and Eildon Hill,
　Fair and too fair you be;
You tell me that the voice is still
　That should have welcomed me.

ANON.

Thomas the Rhymer

True Thomas lay on Huntlie bank,
   A ferlie he spied wi' his e'e,
And there he saw a lady bright
   Come riding down by the Eildon Tree.

Her skirt was o' the grass-green silk,
   Her mantle o' the velvet fine,
At ilka tett of her horse's mane
   Hang fifty siller bells and nine.

True Thomas, he pulled aff his cap,
   And louted low down to his knee:
'All hail, thou mighty Queen of Heaven!
   For thy peer on earth I never did see.'

'O no, O no, Thomas,' she said,
   'That name does not belang to me;
I am but the Queen of fair Elfland,
   That am hither come to visit thee.

'Harp and carp, Thomas,' she said,
   'Harp and carp along wi' me,
And if ye dare to kiss my lips,
   Sure of your body I will be.'

'Betide me weal, betide me woe,
   That weird shall never daunten me.'
Syne he has kissed her rosy lips,
   All underneath the Eildon Tree.

ferlie: marvel   *tett*: lock   *louted*: bowed   *carp*: sing

'Now, ye maun go wi' me,' she said,
  'True Thomas, ye maun go wi' me,
And ye maun serve me seven years,
  Through weal or woe, as may chance to be.'

She mounted on her milk-white steed,
  She's ta'en True Thomas up behind,
And aye whene'er her bridle rung
  The steed flew swifter than the wind.

O they rade on, and farther on –
  The steed gaed swifter than the wind –
Until they reached a desert wide,
  And living land was left behind.

'Light down, light down, now, True Thomas,
  And lean your head upon my knee;
Abide and rest a little space,
  And I will show you ferlies three.

'O see not ye yon narrow road,
  So thick beset with thorns and briers?
That is the path of righteousness,
  Tho' after it but few inquires.

'And see not ye that braid braid road,
  That lies across that lily leven?
That is the path of wickedness,
  Tho' some call it the road to heaven.

'And see not ye that bonnie road
  That winds about the fernie brae?
That is the road to fair Elfland,
  Where thou and I this night maun gae.

leven: lawn

'But, Thomas, ye maun hold your tongue,
    Whatever ye may hear or see,
For, if you speak word in Elfyn land,
    Ye'll ne'er get back to your ain countrie.'

O they rade on, and farther on,
    And they waded through rivers aboon the knee,
And they saw neither sun nor moon,
    But they heard the roaring of the sea.

It was mirk mirk night, and there was nae stern light,
    And they waded thro' red blude to the knee;
For a' the blude that's shed on earth
    Rins thro' the springs o' that countrie.

Syne they came on to a garden green,
    And she pu'd an apple frae a tree;
'Take this for thy wages, True Thomas,
    It will give thee tongue that can never lee.'

'My tongue is mine ain,' True Thomas said;
    'A gudely gift ye wad gie to me!
I neither dought to buy nor sell,
    At fair or tryst where I may be.

'I dought neither speak to prince or peer,
    Nor ask of grace from fair ladie':
'Now hold thy peace,' the lady said,
    'For, as I say, so must it be.'

He has gotten a coat of the even cloth,
    And a pair of shoes of velvet green,
And till seven years were gane and past
    True Thomas on earth was never seen.

stern: star   *mirk*: dark   *dought*: could   *even*: smooth

ROBERT GARIOCH
[1909–82]

Glawmrie

By Earlston, this fourth of June,
   a ferlie I spied wi my ee:
Tammas, frae yon same Ercildoune,
   ken'd-na the like at the Eildon Tree.

In a wee whunstane but-and ben
   I saw a toure flee frae the yird,
And in yon toure I saw twa men,
   In USA by Early Bird.

Smailholm Toure has been upricht
   fu lang. I wannert there-awa
And wunnert if I'd hae a fricht
   whan Smailholm blastit-aff anaa.

What michtna happen on this cleuch
   Sae near owrebye the Eildon Hills?
There's ferlies, even, richt eneuch,
   in Hawick and Gala, at the mills.

But here, inbye the glawmrous howe
   ablow yon triple-bubble brae,
wi rustless blade and rotprufe bow,
   King Arthur's horse and men staund-tae.

I read thae verses frae my buik
   till a black-fac'd yowe, by Smailholm waa.
She gied me an auld-farrant luik,
   Borderer-like, and answered, Baa.

Glawmrie: magic	*yird*: earth	*cleuch*: steep place
ferlie: marvel	*yowe*: ewe	*auld-farrant*: old-fashioned

SIR WALTER SCOTT

[1771–1832]

Edinburgh before Flodden (from *Marmion*)

Early they took Dun-Edin's road,
And I could trace each step they trode;
Hill, brook, nor dell, nor rock, nor stone
Lies on the path to me unknown.
Much might it boast of storied lore;
But, passing such digression o'er,
Suffice it, that their route was laid
Across the furzy hills of Braid.
They passed the glen and scanty rill,
And climbed the opposing bank, until
They gained the top of Blackford Hill.

Blackford! on whose uncultured breast,
 Amongst the broom, the thorn and whin,
A truant boy, I sought the nest,
Or listed, as I lay at rest,
 While rose, on breezes thin,
The murmur of the city crowd,
And, from his steeple jangling loud,
 St Giles's mingling din.
Now, from the summit to the plain,
Waves all the hill with yellow grain;
 And, o'er the landscape as I look,
Nought do I see unchanged remain,
 Save the rude cliffs and chiming brook.
To me they make a heavy moan,
Of early friendships past and gone.

But different far the change has been,
    Since Marmion, from the crown
Of Blackford saw that martial scene
    Upon the bent so brown:
Thousand pavilions, white as snow,
Spread o'er the Boroughmuir below,
    Upland, and dale, and down: –
A thousand did I say? I ween
Thousands on thousands there were seen,
That chequered all the heath between
    The streamlet and the town;
In crossing ranks extending far,
Forming a camp irregular;
Oft giving way, where still there stood
Some reliques of the old oak-wood,
That darkly huge did intervene,
And tame the glaring white with green:
In those extended lines there lay
A martial kingdom's vast array.

Far from Hebudes, dark with rain,
To eastern Lodon's fertile plain,
And from the southern Redswire edge,
To farthest Rosse's rocky ledge;
From west to east, from south to north,
Scotland sent all her warriors forth!
Marmion might hear the mingled hum
Of myriads up the mountain come;
The horses' tramp, and tingling clank,
Where chiefs reviewed their vassal rank,
    And charger's shrilling neigh;
And see the shifting lines advance,
While frequent flashed, from shield and lance,
    The sun's reflected ray.

Thin curling in the morning air,
The wreaths of failing smoke declare,
To embers now the brands decayed,
Where the night-watch their fires had made.
They saw, slow-rolling on the plain,
Full many a baggage cart and wain,
And dire artillery's clumsy car,
By sluggish oxen tugged to war;
And there were Borthwick's Sisters Seven,
And culverins which France had given.
Ill-omened gift! the guns remain
The conqueror's spoil on Flodden plain.

Nor marked they less, where in the air
A thousand streamers flaunted fair;
    Various in shape, device, and hue,
      Green, sanguine, purple, red, and blue,
Broad, narrow, swallow-tailed, and square,
Scroll, pennon, pensil, bandrol, there
    O'er the pavilions flew.
Highest, and midmost, was descried
The royal banner, floating wide;
The staff, a pine-tree strong and straight,
    Pitched deeply in a massive stone,
    Which still in memory is shown,
Yet bent beneath the standard's weight,
Whene'er the western wind unrolled,
With toil, the huge and cumbrous fold,
    And gave to view the dazzling field,
Where, in proud Scotland's royal shield,
The ruddy Lion ramped in gold.

Lord Marmion viewed the landscape bright, –
He viewed it with a chief's delight, –
   Until within him burned his heart,
   And lightning from his eye did part,
     As on the battle-day;
   Such glance did falcon never dart,
     When stooping on his prey.
  'Oh! well, Lord-Lyon, hast thou said,
Thy king from warfare to dissuade
   Were but a vain essay;
For, by Saint-George, were that host mine,
Not power infernal, nor divine,
Should once to peace my soul incline,
Till I had dimmed their armour's shine
   In glorious battle fray!' –
Answered the bard, of milder mood:
   'Fair is the sight, – and yet 'twere good,
   That kings would think withal,
When peace and wealth their land have blessed,
'Tis better to sit still at rest,
   Than rise, perchance to fall.'

Still on the spot Lord Marmion stayed,
For fairer scene he ne'er surveyed.
   When sated with the martial show
   That peopled all the plain below,
   The wandering eye could o'er it go,
   And mark the distant city glow
     With gloomy splendour red;
   For on the smoke-wreaths, huge and slow,
   That round her sable turrets flow,
     The morning beams were shed,
   And tinged them with a lustre proud,
   Like that which streaks a thunder-cloud.
Such dusky grandeur clothed the height,
Where the huge castle holds its state,

And all the steep slope down,
Whose ridgy back heaves to the sky,
Piled deep and massy, close and high,
    Mine own romantic town!
But northward far, with purer blaze,
On Ochil mountains fell the rays,
And as each heathy top they kissed,
It gleamed a purple amethyst.
    Yonder the shores of Fife you saw;
    Here Preston-Bay, and Berwick-Law;
      And, broad between them rolled,
    The gallant Firth the eye might note,
    Whose islands on its bosom float,
      Like emeralds chased in gold.
Fitz-Eustace' heart felt closely pent;
As if to give his rapture vent,
The spur he to his charger lent,
    And raised his bridle-hand,
And, making demi-volte in air,
Cried, 'Where's the coward that would not dare
    To fight for such a land!'
The Lindesay smiled his joy to see;
Nor Marmion's frown repressed his glee.

Thus while they looked, a flourish proud,
Where mingled trump, and clarion loud,
    And fife and kettle-drum,
And sackbut deep and psaltery,
And war-pipe with discordant cry,
And cymbal clattering to the sky,
Making wild music bold and high,
    Did up the mountain come;
The whilst, the bells, with distant chime,
Merrily tolled the hour of prime,
    And thus the Lindesay spoke: –

'Thus clamour still the war-notes when
The King to mass his way has ta'en,
Or to Saint Catherine's of Sienne,
      Or chapel of Saint Rocque.
To you they speak of martial fame;
But me remind of peaceful game,
      When blither was their cheer.
Thrilling in Falkland-woods the air,
In signal none his steed should spare,
But strive which foremost might repair
      To the downfall of the deer.'

'Nor less,' he said, – 'when looking forth,
I view yon Empress of the North
      Sit on her hilly throne;
Her palace's imperial bowers,
Her castle, proof to hostile powers,
Her stately halls, and holy towers –
      Nor less,' he said, 'I moan,
To think what woe mischance may bring,
And how these merry bells may ring
The death-dirge of our gallant King,
      Or, with their larum, call
The burghers forth to watch and ward,
'Gainst southern sack and fires to guard
      Dun-Edin's leaguered wall. –
But not, for my presaging thought,
Dream conquest sure, or cheaply bought.
      Lord Marmion, I say nay: –
God is the guider of the field,
He breaks the champion's spear and shield, –
      But thou thyself shalt say,

When joins yon host in deadly stowre,
That England's dames must weep in bower,
    Her monks the death-mass sing;
For never saw thou such a power
      Led on by such a King.'
And now, down winding to the plain,
The barriers of the camp they gain,
And there they made a stay . . .

JEAN ELLIOT
[1727–1805]

AFTER FLODDEN . . .
The Flowers of the Forest

I've heard the lilting at our yowe-milking,
    Lasses a-lilting before the dawn o' day;
But now they are moaning in ilka green loaning:
    'The Flowers of the Forest are a' wede away.'

At buchts, in the morning, nae blythe lads are scorning;
    The lasses are lonely, and dowie, and wae;
Nae daffin', nae gabbin', but sighing and sabbing:
    Ilk ane lifts her leglen, and hies her away.

In hairst, at the shearing, nae youths now are jeering,
    The bandsters are lyart, and runkled and grey;
At fair or at preaching, nae wooing, nae fleeching:
    The Flowers of the Forest are a' wede away.

At e'en, in the gloaming, nae swankies are roaming
    'Bout stacks wi' the lasses at bogle to play,
But ilk are sits drearie, lamenting her dearie:
    The Flowers of the Forest are a' wede away.

Dule and wae for the order sent our lads to the Border;
    The English, for ance, by guile won the day;
The Flowers of the Forest, that foucht aye the foremost,
    The prime o' our land, are cauld in the clay.

We'll hear nae mair lilting at the yowe-milking,
    Women and bairns are heartless and wae;
Sighing and moaning on ilka green loaning;
    'The Flowers of the Forest are a' wede away.'

yowe: ewe	*loaning*: lane	*wede*: withered
buchts: sheepfolds	*daffin'*: romping	*leglen*: milk-pail
bandsters: binders	*lyart*: grizzled	*fleeching*: flattering
swankies: smart lads	*bogle*: hide-and-seek	*dule*: sorrow

ANON.

The Dowie Houms of Yarrow

Late at een, drinkin' the wine,
    And ere they paid the lawin',
They set a combat them between,
    To fight it in the dawin'.

'O stay at hame, my noble lord!
    O stay at hame, my marrow!
My cruel brother will you betray,
    On the dowie houms o' Yarrow.'

'O fare ye weel, my lady gay!
    O fare ye weel, my Sarah!
For I maun gae, though I ne'er return
    Frae the dowie banks o' Yarrow.'

She kissed his cheek, she kamed his hair,
    As she had done before, O;
She belted on his noble brand,
    An' he's awa to Yarrow.

O he's gane up yon high, high hill –
    I wot he gaed wi' sorrow –
An' in a den spied nine armed men,
    I' the dowie houms o' Yarrow.

'O are ye come to drink the wine,
    As ye hae doon before, O?
Or are ye come to wield the brand,
    On the dowie banks o' Yarrow?'

'I am no come to drink the wine,
    As I hae don before, O,
But I am come to wield the brand,
    On the dowie houms o' Yarrow.'

    marrow: mate   *dowie houms*: sad meadows

Four he hurt, an' five he slew,
  On the dowie houms o' Yarrow,
Till that stubborn knight cam him behind,
  An' ran his body thorrow.

'Gae hame, gae hame, good brother John,
  An' tell your sister Sarah
To come an' lift her noble lord,
  Who's sleepin' sound on Yarrow.'

'Yestreen I dream'd a dolefu' dream;
  I kenned there would be sorrow;
I dream'd I pu'd the heather green,
  On the dowie banks o' Yarrow.'

She gaed up yon high, high hill –
  I wot she gaed wi' sorrow –
An' in a den spied nine dead men,
  On the dowie houms o' Yarrow.

She kissed his cheek, she kamed his hair,
  As oft she did before, O;
She drank the red blood frae him ran,
  On the dowie houms o' Yarrow.

'O haud your tongue, my douchter dear,
  For what needs a' this sorrow?
I'll wed you on a better lord
  Than him you lost on Yarrow.'

'O haud your tongue, my father dear,
  An' dinna grieve your Sarah;
A better lord was never born
  Than him I lost on Yarrow.'

'Tak hame your ousen, take hame your kye,
   For they hae bred our sorrow;
I wiss that they had a' gane mad
   When they cam first to Yarrow.'

SIR RICHARD MAITLAND

[1496–1586]

Aganis the Thieves of Liddesdale

Thae thiefis that stealis and tursis hame,
Ilk ane of them has ane to-name:
    Will of the Lawis,
    Hab of the Shawis;
    To mak bare wa's,
They think na shame.

They spuilye puir men of their packis;
They leif them nocht on bed nor backis;
    Baith hen and cock,
    With reel and rock,
    The Lairdis Jock
All with him takis.

They leif not spindle, spoon nor spit,
Bed, bowster, blanket, serk nor sheet:
    John of the Park
    Ripes kist and ark;
    For all sic wark
He is richt meet.

He is weil kend, John of the Side;
A greater thief did never ride:
    He never tires
    For to break byres;
    Owre muir and mires
Owre gude ane guide.

tursis: carries off
to-name: nickname   *rock*: distaff   *laif*: rest
ripes kist: ransacks chest   *bowster*: bolster

There is ane, callit Clement's Hob,
Fra ilk puir wife reifis her wob,
    And all the laif,
    Whatever they haif:
    The devil resave
Therefor his gob.

Of stouth thoch now they come gude speed
That neither of men nor God has dreid,
    Yit, or I die,
    Some sall them see
    Hing on a tree
Whill they be deid.

gob: belly   *wob*: web   *stouth: robbery*   *whill*: till

ANON.

The Lament of the Border Widow

My love he built me a bonnie bower,
And clad it a' wi' lilye flower;
A brawer bower ye ne'er did see
Than my true love he built for me.

There came a man, by middle day,
He spied his sport, and went away;
And brought the king that very night,
Who brake my bower, and slew my knight.

He slew my knight, to me sae dear;
He slew my knight, and poin'd his gear.
My servants all for life did flee,
And left me in extremetie.

I sewed his sheet, making my maen;
I watched the corpse, myself alane;
I watched his body night and day;
No living creature came that way.

I took his body on my back,
And whiles I gaed and whiles I sat;
I digged a grave and laid him in,
And happ'd him with the sod sae green.

But think na ye my heart was sair
When I laid the moul' on his yellow hair?
O think na ye my heart was wae
When I turned about, awa' to gae?

Nae living man I'll love again,
Since that my lovely knight is slain.
Wi' ae lock o' his yellow hair
I'll chain my heart for evermair.

Drowned in Yarrow

Willy's rare, and Willy's fair,
  And Willy's wondrous bonny;
And Willy hecht to marry me,
  Gin e'er he married ony.

Yestreen I made my bed fu' braid,
  This night I'll make it narrow;
For a' the live-lang winter night
  I lie twin'd of my marrow.

Oh came you by yon water-side,
  Pou'd you the rose or lily?
Or came you by yon meadow green?
  Or saw you my sweet Willy?

She sought him east, she sought him west,
  She sought him braid and narrow;
Syne in the cleaving of a craig
  She found him drown'd in Yarrow.

ANON.

Tweed and Till

Tweed said to Till,
  'What gars ye rin so still?' –
Till said to Tweed,
  'Though ye rin wi' speed,
  And I rin slaw,
Where ye droun ae man,
  I droun twa.'

hecht: promised   *twin'd*: deprived   *marrow*: mate

WILLIAM HENRY OGILVIE
[1869–1964]

The Tweed

Shining and shadowy, verdant-walled
By his banks of spreading beeches,
Thundering over the foaming cauld
And sliding on silver reaches,
Twisting and turning by haugh and lea
Tweed goes down to the windy sea.

Out of the West he takes his way,
And out of the Mosspaul heather
Teviot comes from the hill-mists grey
And the two take hands together,
Laughing comrades that wander down
From abbey to castle, from town to town.

By Tweed as he rolls 'neath the Eildons Three
With the moon in the Melrose arches,
Do the raiders ride again knee to knee,
Trooping down on the English marches?
As he glides where the walls of Dryburgh stand
Does her Great Dead wave him a courtly hand?

By Kelso Bridge at the midnight hour
Stand the monks at the abbey-railing?
Does he hear a guard on the Norham Tower
Through the ghostly moon-mist hailing?
Is there stain of blood where a phantom Till
Creeps from the shadow of Flodden Hill?

Beside him in tiny glen and strath,
With a love that his songs embolden,
Gallant and girl by the river-path
Go down through the grasses golden,
Planning a life that as smooth shall be
As the flow of his waves to the waiting sea.

In the heart of the night go slow, go slow,
As you drift by those dim wraiths sighing;
But, Tweed, for your lovers leap and flow
When the golden sun is shining!
For dead men beckon and grey ghosts call,
But love in its laughter forgets them all!

WILLIAM HENRY OGILVIE
[1869–1964]

Kelso Bridge

There is one spot where memory guides
From time to time my restless heart –
A fair, fair spot, where silver tides
Break on grey piers and drift apart
Round pillars spun with water-weed,
Down channels where the foam is whirled;
So beats my love of home, O Tweed!
Against the barriers of the world!

Rennie's Bridge, Kelso

Sunlit or swept by winter's blast
The old bridge stands, a link between
The Abbey's hoar and wrinkled past
And the young elm-bud's waking green;
The nesting rooks above it wheel
From elm to elm on sable wings;
Beneath it, racing round the reel,
The line upon the bent rod sings.

Across the world hope's bridges bear
The wanderer's never-resting feet,
But peace and rest are mingled where
Earth's fairest rivers, mingling, meet.
On pillars twined with water-weed
Your silver tide is ceaseless hurled;
So beats my love of home, O Tweed!
Against the barriers of the world.

Edinburgh Medley

Braid burn Towlies,
Morningside Swine,
Tipperlinn's the bonnie place
Where a' the leddies dine . . .
Street verse

*

And I forgot the clouded Forth
The gloom that saddens Heaven and Earth
The bitter east, the misty summer
And gray metropolis of the North . . .
Alfred, Lord Tennyson

*

Palace and ruin, bless thee evermore.
Grateful we bow thy gloomy towers before;
For the old Kings of France have found in thee
That melancholy hospitality,
Which in their royal fortune's evil day
Stewarts and Bourbons to each other pay . . .
Victor Hugo

*

God never had a church but there, men say,
The devil a chapel hath raised by some wyles.
I doubted of this saw, till on a day
I westward spied great Edinburgh's Saint Giles . . .
William Drummond of Hawthornden

*

Dante on the Edinburgh People:

In Edinburgh – in Auld Reekie – today
Where 99% of the people might say
In Dante's words . . . 'Tristi fummo
Nell' aer dolce che dal sol s'allegra'
               (Sullen were we
In the sweet air that is gladdened by the sun,
Carrying lazy smoke in our hearts).
                         Hugh MacDiarmid

*

Edinburgh castle, towne and tower,
   God grant ye sink for sin.
And that for the black denner
   Yerl Douglas gat therein.
                     Anon.

ROBERT FERGUSSON
[1750–74]

Auld Reikie

Auld Reikie, wale o' ilka Town
That Scotland kens beneath the Moon;
Where couthy Chiels at E'ening meet
Their bizzing Craigs and Mous to weet;
And blythly gar auld Care gae bye
Wi' blinkit and wi' bleering Eye:
O'er lang frae thee the Muse has been
Sae frisky on the Simmer's Green,
Whan Flowers and Gowans wont to glent
In bonny Blinks upo' the Bent;
But now the Leaves a Yellow die
Peel'd frae the Branches, quickly fly;
And now frae nouther Bush nor Brier
The spreckl'd Mavis greets your ear;
Nor bonny Blackbird skims and roves
To seek his Love in yonder Groves.

Then, Reikie, welcome! Thou canst charm
Unfleggit by the year's Alarm;
Not Boreas that sae snelly blows,
Dare here pap in his angry Nose:
Thanks to our Dads, whase biggin stands
A Shelter to surrounding Lands.

Now Morn, with bonny Purpie-smiles,
Kisses the Air-cock o' St Giles;
Rakin their Ein, the Servant Lasses
Early begin their Lies and Clashes;
Ilk tells her Friend of saddest Distress,
That still she brooks frae scouling Mistress;
And wi' her Joe in Turnpike Stair
She'd rather snuff the stinking Air,
As be subjected to her Tongue,
When justly censur'd in the Wrong.

unfleggit: unfrightened   *biggin*: building

On Stair wi' Tub, or Pat in hand,
The Barefoot Housemaids looe to stand,
That antrin Fock may ken how snell
Auld Reikie will at Morning smell:
Then, with an Inundation big as
The Burn that 'neath the Nore Loch Brig is,
They kindly shower Edina's Roses,
To quicken and regale our Noses.
Now some for this, wi' Satyr's Leesh,
Ha'e gi'en auld Edinburgh a Creesh:
But without Souring nocht is sweet;
The Morning smells that hail our Street,
Prepare, and gently lead the Way
To Simmer canty, braw and gay:
Edina's Sons mair eithly share,
Her Spices and her Dainties rare,
Then he that's never yet been call'd
Aff frae his Plaidie or his Fauld.

Now Stairhead Critics, senseless Fools,
Censure their Aim, and Pride their Rules,
In Luckenbooths, wi' glouring Eye,
Their Neighbours sma'est Faults descry:
If ony Loun should dander there,
Of aukward Gate, and foreign Air,
They trace his Steps, till they can tell
His Pedigree as weel's himsell.

Whan Phœbus blinks wi' warmer Ray
And Schools at Noonday get the play,
Then Bus'ness, weighty Bus'ness comes;
The Trader glours; he doubts, he hums:
The Lawyers eke to Cross repair,
Their Wigs to shaw, and toss an Air;
While busy Agent closely plies,
And a' his kittle Cases tries.

                 antrin: other   *snell*: sharp, cold

Now Night, that's cunzied chief for Fun,
Is wi' her usual Rites begun;
Thro' ilka Gate the Torches blaze,
And Globes send out their blinking Rays.
The usefu' Cadie plies in Street,
To bide the Profits o' his Feet;
For by thir Lads Auld Reikie's Fock
Ken but a Sample, o' the Stock
O' Thieves, that nightly wad oppress,
And make baith Goods and Gear the less.
Near him the lazy Chairman stands,
And wats na how to turn his Hands,
Till some daft Birky, ranting fu',
Has Matters somewhere else to do;
The Chairman willing, gi'es his Light
To Deeds o' darkness and o' Night:

It's never Sax Pence for a Lift
That gars thir Lads wi' fu'ness rift;
For they wi' better Gear are paid,
And Whores and Culls support their Trade.

Near some Lamp-post, wi' dowy Face,
Wi' heavy Ein, and sour Grimace,
Stands she that Beauty lang had kend,
Whoredom her Trade, and Vice her End.
But see wharenow she wuns her Bread
By that which Nature ne'er decreed;
And sings sad Music to the Lugs,
'Mang Burachs o' damn'd Whores and Rogues.
Whane'er we Reputation loss
Fair Chastity's transparent gloss!
Redemption seenil kens the Name,
But a's black Misery and Shame.

cadie: message-boy
burach: cluster

Frae joyous Tavern, reeling drunk,
Wi' fiery Phizz, and Ein half sunk,
Behad the Bruiser, Fae to a'
That in the reek o' Gardies fa':
Close by his Side, a feckless Race
O' Macaronies shew their Face,
And think they're free frae Skaith or Harm,
While Pith befriends their Leader's Arm:
Yet fearfu' aften o' their Maught,
They quatt the Glory o' the Fraught
To this same Warrior wha led
Thae Heroes to bright Honour's Bed;
And aft the hack o' Honour shines
In Bruiser's Face wi' broken Lines:
Of them sad Tales he tells anon,
Whan Ramble and whan Fighting's done;
And, like Hectorian, ne'er impairs
The Brag and Glory o' his Sairs.

Whan Feet in dirty Gutters plash,
And Fock to wale their Fitstaps fash;
At night the Macaroni drunk,
In Pools or Gutters aftimes sunk:
Hegh! what a Fright he now appears,
Whan he his Corpse dejected rears!
Look at that Head, and think if there
The Pomet slaister'd up his Hair!
The Cheeks observe, where now cou'd shine
The scancing Glories o' Carmine?
Ah, Legs! in vain the Silk-worm there
Display'd to View her eidant Care;
For Stink, instead of Perfumes, grow,
And clarty Odours fragrant flow.

fash: trouble   *scancing*: glinting   *eidant*: eager   *clarty*: dirty

Drinking

Clubs

Now some to Porter, some to Punch,
Some to their Wife, and some their Wench,
Retire, while noisy Ten-hours Drum
Gars a' your Trades gae dandring Home.
Now mony a Club, jocose and free,
Gie a' to Merriment and Glee,
Wi' Sang and Glass, they fley the Pow'r
O' Care that wad harrass the Hour:
For Wine and Bacchus still bear down
Our thrawart Fortunes wildest Frown:
It maks you stark, and bauld and brave,
Ev'n whan descending to the Grave.

Now some, in Pandemonium's Shade
Resume the gormandizing Trade;
Where eager Looks, and glancing Ein,
Forespeak a Heart and Stamach keen.
Gang on, my lads; it's lang sin syne
We kent auld Epicurus' Line;
Save you, the Board wad cease to rise,
Bedight wi' Daintiths to the Skies;
And Salamanders cease to swill
The Comforts of a Burning Gill.

But chief, O Cape, we crave thy Aid,
To get our Cares and Poortith laid:
Sincerity, and Genius true,
Of Knights have ever been the due:
Mirth, Music, Porter deepest dy'd,
Are never here to Worth deny'd;
And Health, o' Happiness the Queen,
Blinks bonny, wi' her Smile serene. ✓

Gars: compels   *thrawart*: perverse   *poortith*: poverty

Tho' joy maist Part Auld Reikie owns,
Eftsoons she kens sad sorrow's Frowns;
What Group is yon sae dismal grim,
Wi' Horrid Aspect, cleeding Dim?
Says Death, They're mine, a dowy Crew,
To me they'll quickly pay their last Adieu.

How come mankind, whan lacking Woe,
In Saulie's Face their Heart to show,
As if they were a Clock, to tell
That Grief in them had rung her Bell?
Then, what is Man? why a' this Phraze?
Life's Spunk decay'd, nae mair can blaze.
Let sober Grief alone declare
Our fond Anxiety and Care:
Nor let the Undertakers be
The only waefu' Friends we see.

Come on, my Muse, and then rehearse
The gloomiest Theme in a' your Verse:
In Morning, whan ane keeks about,
Fu' blyth and free frae Ail, nae doubt
He lippens not to be misled
Amang the Regions of the dead:
But straight a painted Corp he sees,
Lang streekit 'neath its Canopies.
Soon, soon will this his Mirth controul,
And send Damnation to his Soul:
Or when the Dead-deal, (awful Shape!)
Makes frighted Mankind girn and gape,
Reflection then his Reason sours,
For the niest Dead-deal may be ours.
Whan Sybil led the Trojan down
To haggard Pluto's dreary Town,
Shapes war nor thae, I freely ween
Cou'd never meet the Soldier's Ein.

Saulie: a hired   *keeks*: looks   *lippen*: trust   *girn*: moan, complain
          mourner

42

Green market

If Kail sae green, or Herbs delight,
Edina's Street attracts the Sight;
Not Covent-garden, clad sae braw,
Mair fouth o' Herbs can eithly shaw:
For mony a Yeard is here sair sought,
That Kail and Cabbage may be bought;
And healthfu' Sallad to regale,
Whan pamper'd wi' a heavy Meal.
Glour up the Street in Simmer Morn,
The Birks sae green, and sweet Brier-thorn,
Wi' sprangit Flow'rs that scent the Gale,
Ca' far awa' the Morning Smell,
Wi' which our Ladies Flow'r-pat's fill'd,
And every noxious Vapour kill'd.
O Nature! canty, blyth and free,
Whare is there Keeking-glass like thee?
Is there on Earth that can compare
Wi' Mary's Shape, and Mary's Air,
Save the empurpl'd Speck, that grows
In the saft Faulds of yonder Rose?
How bonny seems the virgin Breast,
Whan by the Lillies her carest,
And leaves the Mind in doubt to tell
Which maist in Sweets and Hue excel?

    Gillespie's Snuff should prime the Nose
Of her that to the Market goes,
If they wad like to shun the Smells
That buoy up frae markest Cells;
Whare Wames o' Paunches sav'ry scent
To Nostrils gi'e great Discontent.
Now wha in Albion could expect
O' Cleanliness sic great Neglect?

fouth: plenty   *eithly*: easily   *keeking-glass*: mirror   *wame*: belly

43

Nae Hottentot that daily lairs
'Mang Tripe, or ither clarty Wares,
Hath ever yet conceiv'd, or seen
Beyond the Line, sic Scenes unclean.

On Sunday here, an alter'd Scene
O' Men and Manners meets our Ein:
Ane wad maist trow some People chose
To change their Faces wi' their Clo'es,
And fain wad gar ilk Neighbour think
They thirst for Goodness, as for Drink:
But there's an unco Dearth o' Grace,
That has nae Mansion but the Face,
And never can obtain a Part
In benmost Corner of the Heart.
Why should Religion make us sad,
If good frae Virtue's to be had?
Na, rather gleefu' turn your Face;
Forsake Hypocrisy, Grimace;
And never have it understood
You fleg Mankind frae being good.

In Afternoon, a' brawly buskit,
The Joes and Lasses loe to frisk it:
Some tak a great delight to place
The modest Bongrace o'er the Face;
Tho' you may see, if so inclin'd,
The turning o' the Leg behind.
Now Comely-Garden, and the Park,
Refresh them, after Forenoon's Wark;
Newhaven, Leith or Canon-mills,
Supply them in their Sunday's Gills;
Whare Writers aften spend their Pence,
To stock their Heads wi' Drink and Sense.

buskit: clothed, adorned

44

While dandring Cits delight to stray
To Castlehill, or Public Way,
Whare they nae other Purpose mean,
Than that fool Cause o' being seen;
Let me to Arthur's Seat pursue,
Whare bonny Pastures meet the View;
And mony a wild-lorn Scene accrues,
Befitting Willie Shakespeare's Muse:
If Fancy there would join the Thrang,
The desart Rocks and Hills amang,
To Echoes we should lilt and play,
And gie to Mirth the lee-lang Day.

Or shou'd some canker'd biting Show'r
The Day and a' her Sweets deflour,
To Holy-rood-house let me stray,
And gie to musing a' the Day;
Lamenting what auld Scotland knew
Bien Days for ever frae her View:
O Hamilton, for shame! the Muse
Would pay to thee her couthy Vows,
Gin ye wad tent the humble Strain
And gie's our Dignity again:
For O, waes me! the Thistle springs
In Domicile of ancient Kings,
Without a Patriot to regrete
Our Palace, and our ancient State.

Blest Place! whare Debtors daily run,*
To rid themselves frae Jail and Dun;
Here, tho' sequester'd frae the Din
That rings Auld Reikie's Waas within,
Yet they may tread the sunny Braes,
And brook Apollo's cheery rays;

* The precincts of Holyrood-house were a debtors' sanctuary.

45

Glour frae St Anthon's grassy Hight,
O'er Vales in Simmer Claise bedight,
Nor ever hing their Head, I ween,
Wi' jealous Fear o' being seen.
May I, whenever Duns come nigh,
And shake my Garret wi' their Cry,
Scour here wi' Haste, Protection get,
To screen mysell frae them and Debt;
To breathe the Bliss of open Sky,
And Simon Fraser's Bolts defy.

Arthur's Seat

Now gin a Lown should ha'e his Clase
In Thread-bare Autumn o' their Days,
St Mary, Brokers' Guardian Saint,
Will satisfy ilk Ail and Want;
For mony a hungry Writer, there
Dives down at Night, wi' cleading bare,
And quickly rises to the View
A Gentleman, perfyte and new.
Ye rich Fock, look no wi' Disdain
Upo' this ancient Brokage Lane!
For naked Poets are supplied,
With what you to their Wants deny'd.

St Mary's St

Peace to thy Shade, thou wale o' Men,
Drummond! Relief to Poortith's Pain:
To thee the greatest Bliss we owe;
And Tribute's Tear shall grateful flow:
The Sick are cur'd, the Hungry fed,
And Dreams of Comfort tend their Bed:
As lang as Forth weets Lothians Shore,
As lang's on Fife her billows roar,
Sae lang shall ilk whase Country's dear,
To thy Remembrance gie a Tear.

Drummond.

gin: if   *cleading*: clothing   *Lown*: loon, chap

By thee Auld Reikie thrave, and grew
Delightfu' to her Childers View:
Nae mair shall Glasgow Striplings threap
Their City's Beauty and its Shape,
While our New City spreads around
Her bonny Wings on Fairy Ground.

    But Provosts now that ne'er afford
The smaest dignity to lord,
Ne'er care tho' every scheme gae wild
That Drummond's sacred hand has cull'd:
The spacious Brig neglected lies,
Tho' plagu'd wi' pamphlets, dunn'd wi' cries;
They heed not tho' destruction come
To gulp us in her gaunting womb.
Oh shame! that safety canna claim
Protection from a provost's name,
But hidden danger lies behind
To torture and to fleg the mind;
I may as weel bid Arthur's Seat
To Berwick-Law make gleg retreat,
As think that either will or art
Shall get the gate to win their heart;
For Politics are a' their mark,
Bribes latent, and corruption dark:
If they can eithly turn the pence,
Wi' city's good they will dispense;
Nor care tho' a' her sons were lair'd
Ten fathom i' the auld kirk-yard.

threap: insist on, boast of   *gaunting*: yawning   *gleg*: quick

To sing yet meikle does remain,
Undecent for a modest strain;
And since the poet's daily bread is
The favour of the Muse or ladies,
He downa like to gie offence
To delicacy's bonny sense;
Therefore the stews remain unsung,
And bawds in silence drop their tongue.

Reikie, farewel! I ne'er cou'd part
Wi' thee but wi' a dowy heart;
Aft frae the Fifan coast I've seen,
Thee tow'ring on thy summit green;
So glowr the saints when first is given
A fav'rite keek o' glore and heaven;
On earth nae mair they bend their ein,
But quick assume angelic mein;
So I on Fife wad glowr no more,
But gallop'd to Edina's shore.

ROBERT GARIOCH
[1909–82]

At Robert Fergusson's Grave
October 1962

Canongait kirkyaird in the failing year
is auld and grey, the wee roseirs are bare,
five gulls leam white agin the dirty air:
why are they here? There's naething for them here.

    Why are we here oursels? We gaither near
the grave. Fergusons mainly, quite a fair
turn-out, respectfu, ill at ease, we stare
at daith – there's an address – I canna hear.

    Aweill, we staund bareheidit in the haar,
murning a man that gaed back til the pool
twa-hunner year afore our time. The glaur

    that haps his banes glowres back. Strang, present dool
ruggs at my hairt. Lichtlie this gin ye daur:
here Robert Burns knelt and kissed the mool.

glaur: soft mud	*roseirs*: rose-bushes	*dool*: grief	*mool*: earth
	lichtlie: despise	*ruggs*: pulls	on grave

ARTHUR HENRY HALLAM
[1811–33]

Edinburgh

Even thus, methinks, a city reared should be,
  Yea, an imperial city, that might hold
Five times a hundred noble towns in fee,
  And either with their might of Babel old,
Or the rich Roman pomp of empery
  Might stand compare, highest in arts enroll'd,
Highest in arms; brave tenement for the free,
  Who never crouch to thrones, or sin for gold.
Thus should her towers be raised – with vicinage
  Of clear bold hills, that curve her very streets,
As if to vindicate, 'mid choicest seats
Of art, abiding Nature's majesty,
And the broad sea beyond, in calm or rage
Chainless alike, and teaching Liberty.

Edinburgh from Calton Hill (c. 1880)

ROBERT LOUIS STEVENSON
[1850–94]

Edinburgh from the South Seas

The tropics vanish, and meseems that I,
From Halkerside, from topmost Allermuir,
Or steep Caerketton, dreaming gaze again.
Far set in fields and woods, the town I see
Spring gallant from the shallows of her smoke,
Cragged, spired and turreted, her virgin fort
Beflagged. About, on seaward-drooping hills,
New folds of city glitter. Last, the Forth
Wheels ample waters set with sacred isles,
And populous Fife smokes with a score of towns.
There, on the sunny frontage of a hill,
Hard by the house of kings, repose the dead,
My dead, the ready and the strong of word.
Their works, the salt-encrusted, still survive;
The sea bombards their founded towers; the night
Thrills pierced with their strong lamps. The artificers,
One after one, here in this grated cell,
Where the rain erases and the rust consumes,
Fell upon lasting silence. Continents
And continental oceans intervene;
A sea uncharted, on a lampless isle,
Environs and confines their wandering child
In vain. The voice of generations dead
Summons me, sitting distant, to arise,
My numerous footsteps nimbly to retrace,
And, all mutation over, stretch me down
In that denoted city of the dead.

ANON.

The Souters of Selkirk

Up wi' the souters of Selkirk,
   And down wi' the Earl of Home;
And up wi' a' the braw lads
   Wha sew the single-soled shoon!
O! fye upon yellow and yellow,
   And fye upon yellow and green;
But up wi' the true-blue and scarlet,
   And up wi' the single-soled shoon.

Up wi' the souters of Selkirk –
   Up wi' the lingle and last!
There's fame wi' the days that's coming,
   And glory wi' them that are past:
Up wi' the souters of Selkirk –
   Lads that are trusty and leal;
And up wi' the men of the Forest,
   And down wi' the Merse to the Deil!

O! mitres are made for noddles,
   But feet they are made for shoon:
And fame is as sib to Selkirk
   As light is true to the mune:
There sits a souter in Selkirk
   Wha sings as he draws his thread –
There's gallant souters in Selkirk
   As lang's there's water in Tweed.

souter: shoemaker   *leal*: loyal   *sib*: native

ANON.

Lammermuir

Happy the craw
   That biggs in the Trotten shaw,
And drinks o' the Water o' Dye –
   For nae mair may I.

SIR WALTER SCOTT

[1771–1832]

Blue Bonnets over the Border

March, march, Ettrick and Teviotdale,
    Why the deil dinna ye march forward in order?
March, march, Eskdale and Liddesdale,
    All the Blue Bonnets are bound for the Border.
        Many a banner spread,
        Flutters above your head,
    Many a crest that is famous in story,
        Mount and make ready then,
        Sons of the mountain glen,
    Fight for the Queen and the old Scottish glory!

Come from the hills where the hirsels are grazing,
    Come from the glen of the buck and the roe;
Come to the crag where the beacon is blazing,
    Come with the buckler, the lance and the bow.
        Trumpets are sounding,
        War-steeds are bounding,
    Stand to your arms then, and march in good order,
        England shall many a day
        Tell of the bloody fray,
    When the Blue Bonnets came over the Border!

LADY JOHN SCOTT

[1810–1900]

Ettrick

When we first rade down Ettrick,
Our bridles were ringing, our hearts were dancing,
The waters were singing, the sun was glancing,
An' blithely our voices rang out thegither,
As we brushed the dew frae the blooming heather,
    When we first rade down Ettrick.

When we next rade down Ettrick
The day was dying, the wild birds calling,
The wind was sighing, the leaves were falling,
An' silent an' weary, but closer thegither,
We urged our steeds thro' the faded heather,
    When we next rade down Ettrick.

When I last rade down Ettrick,
The winds were shifting, the storm was waking,
The snow was drifting, my heart was breaking,
For we never again were to ride thegither,
In sun or storm on the mountain heather,
    When I last rade down Ettrick.

SIR WALTER SCOTT

[1771–1832]

November, Ettrick Forest

November's sky is chill and drear,
November's leaf is red and sear:
Late, gazing down the steepy linn,
That hems our little garden in,
Low in its dark and narrow glen,
You scarce the rivulet might ken,
So thick the tangled green-wood grew,
So feeble trilled the streamlet through:
Now, murmuring hoarse, and frequent seen
Through bush and brier, no longer green,
An angry brook, it sweeps the glade,
Brawls over rock and wild cascade,
And, foaming brown with doubled speed,
Hurries its waters to the Tweed.

No longer Autumn's glowing red
Upon our Forest hills is shed;
No more, beneath the evening beam,
Fair Tweed reflects their purple gleam;
Away hath passed the heather-bell,
That bloomed so rich on Neidpath-fell;
Sallow his brow, and russet bare
Are now the sister-heights of Yair.
The sheep, before the pinching heaven,
To sheltered dale and down are driven,
Where yet some faded herbage pines,
And yet a watery sunbeam shines:
In meek despondency they eye
The withered sward and wintry sky,

And far beneath their summer hill,
Stray sadly by Glenkinnon's rill:
The shepherd shifts his mantle's fold,
And wraps him closer from the cold;
His dogs no merry circles wheel,
But, shivering, follow at his heel;
A cowering glance they often cast,
As deeper moans the gathering blast . . .

WILLIAM WORDSWORTH
[1770–1850]

Yarrow Visited

And is this – Yarrow? – *This* the Stream
Of which my fancy cherished,
So faithfully, a waking dream?
An image that hath perished!
O that some Minstrel's harp were near,
To utter notes of gladness,
And chase this silence from the air,
That fills my heart with sadness!

Yet why? – a silvery current flows
With uncontrolled meanderings;
Nor have these eyes by greener hills
Been soothed, in all my wanderings.
And, through her depths, Saint Mary's Lake
Is visibly delighted;
For not a feature of those hills
Is in the mirror slighted.

A blue sky bends o'er Yarrow vale,
Save where that pearly whiteness
Is round the rising sun diffused,
A tender hazy brightness;
Mild dawn of promise! that excludes
All profitless dejection;
Though not unwilling here to admit
A pensive recollection.

Where was it that the famous Flower
Of Yarrow Vale lay bleeding?
His bed perchance was yon smooth mound
On which the herd is feeding:
And haply from this crystal pool,
Now peaceful as the morning,
The Water-wraith ascended thrice –
And gave his doleful warning.

Delicious is the Lay that sings
The haunts of happy Lovers,
The path that leads them to the grove,
The leafy grove that covers:
And Pity sanctifies the Verse
That paints, by strength of sorrow,
The unconquerable strength of love;
Bear witness, rueful Yarrow!

But thou, that didst appear so fair
To fond imagination,
Dost rival in the light of day
Her delicate creation:
Meek loveliness is round thee spread,
A softness still and holy;
The grace of forest charms decayed,
And pastoral melancholy.

That Region left, the Vale unfolds
Rich groves of lofty stature,
With Yarrow winding through the pomp
Of cultivated nature;
And, rising from those lofty groves,
Behold a Ruin hoary!
The shattered front of Newark's Towers,
Renowned in Border story.

Fair scenes for childhood's opening bloom,
For sportive youth to stray in;
For manhood to enjoy his strength;
And age to wear away in!
Yon Cottage seems a bower of bliss,
A covert for protection
Of tender thoughts, that nestle there,
The brood of chaste affection.

How sweet, on this autumnal day,
The wild-wood fruits to gather,
And on my True-love's forehead plat
A crest of blooming heather!
And what if I enwreathed my own!
'Twere no offence to reason;
The sober Hills thus deck their brows
To meet the wintry season.

I see – but not by sight alone,
Loved Yarrow, have I won thee;
A ray of Fancy still survives –
Her sunshine plays upon thee!
Thy ever-youthful waters keep
A course of lively pleasure;
And gladsome notes my lips can breathe,
Accordant to the measure.

The vapours linger round the Heights,
They melt, and soon must vanish;
One hour is theirs, nor more is mine –
Sad thought, which I would banish,
But that I know, where'er I go,
Thy genuine image, Yarrow!
Will dwell with me – to heighten joy,
And cheer my mind in sorrow.

ROGER QUIN

[1850–1925]

The Borderland

From the moorland and the meadows
To this city of the shadows,
Where I wander old and lonely, comes the call I understand;
In clear, soft tones enthralling,
It is calling – calling – calling –
'Tis the Spirit of the Open from the dear old Borderland!

Ah that call! who can gainsay it?
To hear is to obey it;
I must leave the bustling city to the busy city men –
Leave behind its feverish madness,
Its scenes of sordid sadness;
And drink the unpolluted air of Yarrow once again!

For the grim, huge city daunts me,
Its wail of sorrow haunts me –
A nameless Atom tossed amidst the human surf that beats!
For ever and for ever,
In a frenzy of endeavour,
Along the cruel barriers of its never-ending streets!

I shall leave it in the morning –
Just slip out without a warning,
Save a hand-clasp to the friend who knows the call that lures me on;
In the city's clang and clatter
One old man the less won't matter;
And no one here will say me nay, or care that I am gone.

What tho' my wallet's meagre?
That won't quell my spirit eager –
Like careless-hearted Goldsmith when he wandered by the Po,
Whichever way I turn me,
My simple flute will earn me
In the kindly Border country, food and shelter as I go.

I shall see old Neidpath hoary,
With its dim, romantic story,
And soon have glimpses through the trees of ghostly grey Traquair;
And in my happy wand'ring
Adown the Tweed's meand'ring
Shall note the Peel, and Ashiestiel, and onward to the Yair.

By Caddonfoot I'll linger –
It has charms to stay the singer –
And from the bridge a painter's dream of beauty then I'll see;
But I'll leave it there behind me,
Ere the evening shadows find me
Passing the vines at Clovenfords to haunted Torwoodlee.

Gala Water shall not hold me –
Tho' its mem'ries fair enfold me –
Nor many-gabled Abbotsford, so stately and so still;
For I'll hasten to the vision
Of a valley fair, Elysian,
And gaze on Scotland's Eden from the spur of Gala Hill.

Ah me! shall I recapture
The early joyous rapture
Which shook my being's pulses when that scene first met my eye?
. Steeped in old Border story
It stretched in radiant glory,
To where the filmy Cheviots hung along the southern sky!

Fair Dryburgh and Melrose,
Touched by the Wizard's spell, rose,
And Bemersyde, and Leaderfoot, and Elwyn's Fairy Dene:
The Tweed serenely gliding,
Now seen – now coyly hiding,
While Eildon raised his triple crest, and sentinelled the scene!

The spell – the dream is over:
I awake, but to discover
The city's rush – the jostling crowds – the din on every hand;
But, on my ear soft falling,
I can hear the curlews calling,
And I know that soon I'll see them in the dear old Borderland!

JOHN LEYDEN

[1775–1811]

Teviotdale

Again, beside this silver rivulet's shore,
With green and yellow moss-flowers mottlied o'er,
Beneath a shivering canopy reclined,
Of aspen leaves, that wave without a wind,
I love to lie, when lulling breezes stir
The spiry cones that tremble on the fir,
Or wander mid the dark-green fields of broom,
When peers, in scattered tufts, the yellow bloom,
Or trace the path, with tangling furze o'er-run;
When bursting seed-bells crackle in the sun,
And pittering grass-hoppers, confusedly shrill,
Pipe giggily along the glowing hill . . .

ANON.

Juvenis and Piscator

Juv: Canny Fisher Jamie, comin' hame at e'en,
·   Canny Fisher Jamie, whaur hae ye been?

Pisc: Mony lang miles, laddie, ower the Kips sae green.

Juv: Fishing Leithen Water?

Pisc: Nay, laddie, nay.
Just a wee burnie rinnin' doun a brae,
Fishin' a wee burnie nae bigger than a sheugh.

Juv: Gat ye mony troots, Jamie?

Pisc: I gat eneugh –
Eneugh tae buy my baccy, snuff and pickle tea,
An' lea' me tippence for a gill, and that's eneugh
    for me.

sheugh: ditch

JOHN BUCHAN
[1875–1940]

Fisher Jamie

Puir Jamie's killed. A better lad
   Ye wadna find tae busk a flee
Or burn a pule or wield a gad
   Frae Berwick tae the Clints' o' Dee.

And noo he's in a happier land –
   It's Gospel truith and Gospel Law
That Heaven's yett maun open stand
   To folk that for their country fa'.

But Jamie will be ill to mate;
   He lo'ed nae music, kenned nae tunes
Except the sang o' Tweed in spate,
   Or Talla loupin' ower its linns.

I sair misdoubt that Jamie's heid
   A croun o' gowd will never please;
He liked a kep o' dacent tweed
   Whaur he could stick his casts o' flees.

If Heaven is a' that man can dream
   And a' that honest herts can wish,
It maun provide some muirland stream,
   For Jamie dreamed o' nocht but fish.

And weel I wot he'll up and speir
   In his bit blate and canty way,
Wi' kind apostles standin' near
   Whae in their time were fishers tae.

busk: dress	*yett*: gate	*loupin'*: leaping
gad: gaff	*blate and canty*: shy and friendly	*speir*: ask

He'll offer back his gowden croun
   And in its place a rod he'll seek,
And bashfu'-like his herp lay doun
   And speir a leister and a cleek.

For Jims had aye a poachin' whim;
   He'll sune grow tired, wi' lawfu' flee
Made frae the wings o' Cherubim
   O' castin' ower the Crystal Sea.

I picter him at gloamin' tide
   Steekin' the back-door o' his hame
And hastin' to the waterside
   To play again the auld auld game;

And syne wi saumon on his back
   Catch't clean against the Heavenly law,
And Heavenly byliffs on his track,
   Gaun linkin' doun some Heavenly shaw.

leister: salmon-spear   *steekin'*: shutting   *linkin'*: stealing   *shaw*: wood

Vale of Tweed, Melrose

STEWART CONN
[b. 1936]

End of Season, Drumelzier

Scarcely discernible, the line tautens
Against the current, then sweeps downstream.
The rod-tip shifts, dislodging a thin
Gleam of light. I spool in, cast again.

So the season ends. In near darkness
I try to reach the rise.
Something jumps. The circles
Are absorbed. Night closes in.

I stumble from the luminescent Tweed,
And trudge by moonlight to the farm.
Then home: waders discarded, I concentrate
On the winding road; watch hedgerows pass,

Sheer banks; branches like weed, overhead.
Sedgeflies smudge the screen. I bear left
Towards row upon row of lights that never meet.
In under an hour, I am crossing Princes Street.

So the close of each trout season
Brings its own desperation
To make up for lost days; a trek
To the river, a casting more frantic

Than judged. In life and love too, take care
To make the most of time before,
Darkness encroaching, it is too late
For anything but the final onslaught.

[1874–1955]

Colinton

Silence herself made lovely Colinton,
Ringing her round with battlements of trees.
She is a village of the Pyrenees
Torn from the Iberian hills, and plunged upon
These lofty Lothian leas,
Rising and bending, valley-wending,
Stream-seeking, serpentine of lanes,
A little city of moraines.
Ever to deeper peace descending.
She looks up to a roof of green
Like a white town in Thrasymene.
Her slim Italian spire conceives
A thought of Tuscany in leaves.
Her rugged hillside magic falls like trance,
A dreamy cataract of copse and scar,
Wild as the vision of a lost romance,
Down to her heart, where singing waters are.

Ah, if I sang a hundred years
I might not do her greenness praise!
Her elms have been my friends in days
I felt my closest friends were fears.
Oft-times have passed mysterious sympathies
Between my spirit and her whispering trees.

Ballantyne's Close, Grassmarket, Edinburgh (c. 1850)

[b. 1910]

Edinburgh Courtyard in July

Hot light is smeared as thick as paint
On these ramshackle tenements. Stones smell
   Of dust. Their hoisting into quaint
Crowsteps, corbels, carved with fool and saint,
Hold fathoms of heat, like water in a well.

   Cliff-dwellers have poked out from their
High cave-mouths brilliant rags on drying-lines;
   They hang still, dazzling in the glare,
And lead the eye up, ledge by ledge, to where
A chimney's tilted helmet winks and shines.

   And water from a broken drain
Splashes a glassy hand out in the air
   That breaks in an unbraiding rain
And falls still fraying, to become a stain
That spreads by footsteps, ghosting everywhere.

HENRY JOHNSTONE
[*fl* 1890]

On the Dean Bridge in June

White lamps the chestnut-tree adorn,
    The lilacs and the golden-rain,
The snowy and the rosy thorn
    Are rife with blossom once again.

Though on this pleasance June bestows
    His gifts with such a lavish hand,
Not like a beggar hence he goes;
    His largesse reaches all the land.

But from the Bridge I lean and look,
    Going and coming, late and soon,
And thank God for this flowery nook,
    The paradise of peerless June.

Snow on the Ochils

Snow on the Ochils and sun on the snow,
Ha, my brave Winter, if you can bestow,
Out of your penury treasures like these,
Never grudge Summer her blossoms and bees.

Gardens in glory and balms in the breeze,
Ah, pretty Summer, e'en boast as you please,
Sweet are your gifts; but to Winter we owe
Snow on the Ochils and sun on the snow.

STEWART CONN

[b. 1936]

New Town, Autumn

October ends. Against my study wall
the rose-hips shrivel. The central

heating is like leaves shifting
behind the skirting.

The boys' woollens and long
stockings are laid out for the morning.

Since the hour went back there has been
mist, incessant rain.

At dusk the New Town
comes into its own:

a cat at each corner, shady permutations
of wives and lovers gliding through its lanes.

In bed, we cling to one another
and prepare for a long winter.

NORMAN MACCAIG
[b. 1910]

Drop-Out in Edinburgh

I steal nothing from you.
I am your incandescent heir.
You bequeath me my incandescence.

City of everywhere, broken necklace in the sun,
you are caves of guilt, you are pinnacles of jubilation.
Your music is a filigree of drumming.
You frown into the advent of heavenly hosts.
Your iron finger shatters sad suns –
they multiply in scatters, they swarm
on fizzing roofs. When the sea
breathes gray over you, you become
one lurking-place, one shifting of nowheres –
in it are warpipes and genteel pianos
and the sawing voices of lawyers. Your buildings
are broken memories, your streets
lost hopes – but you shrug off time, you set your face
against all that is not you.

I am your incandescent heir.
I am your morning side, I am your golden acre.
Your windows glitter me, the sheen
on your pigeons' breasts is me.
I glide through your dark streets like phosphorus.

[b. 1910]

Milne's Bar

Cigarette smoke floated
in an Eastern way
a yard above the slopped tables.

The solid man thought
nothing could hurt him
as long as he didn't show it –

a stoicism of a kind. I
was inclined to agree with him,
having had a classical education.

To prove it, he went on telling
of terrible things that had
happened to him –

so boringly, my mind
skipped away among the glasses
and floated, in an Eastern way,

a yard above the slopped
table; when it looked down,
the solid man

was crying into his own mouth.
I caught sight of myself
in a mirror

and stared, rather admiring
the look of suffering
in my middle-aged eyes.

HUGH MACDIARMID
[1892–1978]

Old Wife in High Spirits
In an Edinburgh pub

An auld wumman cam' in, a mere rickle of banes, in a faded black
    dress
And a bonnet wi' beads o' jet rattlin' on it;
A puir-lookin' cratur, you'd think she could haurdly ha'e had less
Life left in her and still lived, but dagonit.

He gied her a stiff whisky – she was nervous as a troot
And could haurdly haud the tumbler, puir cratur;
Syne he gied her anither, joked wi' her, and anither, and syne
Wild as the whisky up cam' her nature.

The rod that struck water frae the rock in the desert
Was naething to the life that sprang oot o' her;
The dowie auld soul was twinklin' and fizzin' wi' fire;
You never saw ocht sae souple and kir.

Like a sackfu' o' monkeys she was, and her lauchin'
Loupit up whiles to incredible heights;
Wi' ane owre the eight her temper changed and her tongue
Flew juist as the forkt lichtnin' skites.

The heich-skeich auld cat was fair in her element;
Wanton as a whirlwind, and shairly better that way
Than a' crippen thegither wi' laneliness and cauld
Like a foretaste o' the graveyaird clay.

Some folk nae doot'll condemn gie'in' a guid spree
To the puir dune body and raither she endit her days
Like some auld tashed copy o' the Bible yin sees
On a street book-barrow's tippenny trays,

kir: cheerful	*loupit*: leapt	*skites*: jumps
heich-skeich: crazy	*crippen*: gathered	

A' I ken is weel-fed and weel-put-on though they be
Ninety per cent o' respectable folk never hae
As muckle life in their creeshy carcases frae beginnin' to end
As kythed in that wild auld carline that day!

kythed: rose up   *carline*: old woman,   *creeshy*: fat
hag

GEORGE BARKER
[b. 1913]

Scottish Bards and an English Reviewer

And in the Abbotsford
Like gabbing asses
They scale the heights
Of Ben-Parnassus
And on each shoulder
Like a rowan
A chip that goes on
Growing growing
Till every motion
Of the mind
(Not all originate
Behind)
Looks like rags
Blown amiss
Into the branches
Of prejudice.
The dark and feral
Gaelic fancy
Mysterious
As necromancy
Calling up from
Past and present
Nothing that is
Very pleasant,
And over all
The tragic scene
Of what is not
And what has been,
The cannibalistic
Sawney Bean
Stands chewing on
An arm or leg
Or sucking a testicle

Like an egg.
And strutting up and
Down the Mile
The uncrowned Laird
Of Scottish style
– Is it a Scott
He's walking with? –
The only kilted
Kiwi – Smith.
There's a Lindsay this
And a Lindsay that
There's a Craig tit
And a Craig tat
There's a Robert Tweedle
And a Robert Tum
And a Campbell looking
A bit glum
– They are all there
Chests stuck out
Pouring down gallons
Of Irish stout
And with the whisky
Flowing free
Damning the Sassanach
Lickpenny.
'Why dinna ye
Lairn frae us?
Canna ye see
We're marvellous?
Without so much as
One word written
We're the finest poets
In all Britain.
Stand me a pint
Of the singing stuff
An' I'll shoot ye an epic straight

Off me cuff.
Och, if only I still had
Me little knife
I'd cut us off at
The Forth of Fife
Or maybe I mean
The Fife of Forth
Weel, dinna fash,
Anywhere north
Of the bluidy border
That's atween
All Scottish order
And Putney Green.'
And Time draws on
And Time draws near
As we drown ten beers
In some more beer,
Till in the dim
Illumination
Of alcoholic
Stimulation
We see that all
The woes of the Scot
Ensue from God knows
Only what
But definitely
They do not
Arise from any
Fault at all
Native north of
The Roman Wall.
The minstrels flash
The witty claymore
And we all mean less
As we all say more
Till the bards sink

In a tartan clamour
Like their heroes under
The auction hammer
But from the floor
Where they lie in rows
Arises the story
Of Scotland's woes
As the voice of the bard
Sighs out of its cup:
'Why the hell dinna ye
Help me up?'
O Caledonia
Fair and wild
Bitter as bitter
Mild as mild
But the blood of a Scot
When he's had a dram
Couldn't be stopped
By Boulder Dam
So it's 'Out of me way
Ye lesser species
I say what I think o' ye
In me faeces.
Where oh where
Would this whole warruld be
If it wasn't for Rabbie
Burns and me?'
Then the stars spey out
Over Princes Street
And not one of us left
On his own feet
As we float away
Down the Royal Mile
Swearing in rime
Swabbed in style
And proud as MacPunch

All the while –
Till faintly as
We disappear
A Grieving Pibroch
Assails my ear:
'I tell you, mon,
This universe
Will go on getting
Worse and worse
Till they pass a law
That only (sic) Scotch
Is allowed to think
Or wear a watch
Or take a drink.
For every other
Earthly nation
Can tell the time
From their subjugation
And as for ratio-
cination,
Why, any fool who's
Not too cliquey
Knows it started
In Auld Reekie,
And every other
Heathen knows
A thristle (Scottish)
Outsings a rose.'
'And still an' all
And all the same'
Soloes the lyre
Of Jock S Graham
'Now Dylan's dead an'
I survive,
Why, mon, I'm the only
Scald alive.'

Then the moon, like the truth,
Rose over the fog
Of the tartan night,
And sick as a dog
I made my way
To a sottish bed
And a Scottish day.

ROBERT GARIOCH
[1909–82]

Embro to the Ploy

In simmer, whan aa sorts foregether
in Embro to the ploy,
fowk seek out friens to hae a blether,
or faes they'd fain annoy;
smorit wi British Railways' reek
frae Glesca or Glen Roy
or Wick, they come to hae a week
of cultivatit joy,
      or three,
in Embro to the ploy.

Americans wi routh of dollars,
wha drink our whisky neat,
wi Sasunachs and Oxford Scholars
are eydent for the treat
of music sedulously high-tie
at thirty-bob a seat;
Wop opera performed in Eytie
to them's richt up their street,
      they say,
in Embro to the ploy.

Furthgangan Embro folk come hame
for three weeks in the year,
and find Auld Reekie no the same,
fu sturrit in a steir.
The stane-faced biggins whaur they froze
and suppit puirshous leir
of cultural cauld-kale and brose
see cantraips unco queer
      thae days
in Embro to the ploy.

[handwritten marginal note: Festival decoration]

[handwritten marginal note: Usher Hall]

ploy: frolic	*smorit*: smothered	*eydent*: eager	*furthgangan*: exiled
routh: plenty	*steir*: hurly-burly	*puirshous*: precious	*leir*: learning

The tartan tred wad gar ye lauch;
nae problem is owre teuch.
Your surname needna end in -*och*;
they'll cleik ye up the cleuch.
A puckle dollar bills will aye
preive Hiram Teufelsdrockh
a septary of Clan McKay,
it's maybe richt eneuch,
                    verfluch!
in Embro to the ploy.

The auld High Schule, whaur monie a skelp
of triple-tonguit tawse
has gien a hyst-up and a help
towards Doctorates of Laws,
nou hears, for Ramsay's cantie rhyme,
loud pawmies of applause
frae folk that pey a pund a time
to sit on wudden raws
                    gey hard
in Embro to the ploy.

The haly kirk's Assembly-haa
nou fairly coups the creel
wi Lindsay's Three Estaitis, braw
devices of the Deil.
About our heids the satire stots
like hailstanes till we reel;
the bawrs are in auld-farrant Scots,
it's maybe jist as weill,
                    imphm,
in Embro to the ploy.

cleik: hook	*cleuch*: steep place	*skelp*: smack	*tawse*: strap
coups: upsets	*creel*: basket	*stots*: bounces	*bawrs*: jokes

The Epworth Haa wi wunner did
behold a piper's bicker;
wi *hadarid* and *hindarid*
the air gat thick and thicker.
Cumha na Cloinne pleyed on strings
torments a piper quicker
to get his dander up, by jings,
than thirty u.p. liquor,
			hooch aye!
in Embro to the ploy.

The North British Embro Whigs
that stayed in Charlotte Square,
they fairly wad hae tined their wigs
to see the Stuarts there,
the bleidan Earl of Moray and aa
weill-pentit and gey bare;
Our Queen and Princess, buskit braw,
enjoyed the hale affair
			(see Press)
in Embro to the ploy.

Whan day's anomalies are cled
in decent shades of nicht,
the Castle is transmogrified
by braw electric licht.
The toure that bields the Bruce's croun
presents an unco sicht
mair sib to Wardour Street nor Scone,
wae's me for Scotland's micht,
			says I
in Embro to the ploy.

tine: lose   *bield*: shelter

A happening, incident, or splore
affrontit them that saw
a thing they'd never seen afore –
in the McEwan Haa:
a lassie in a wheelie-chair
wi naething on at aa.
jist like my luck! I wasna there.
it's no the thing ava,
                    tut-tut,
in Embro to the ploy.

The Café Royal and Abbotsford
are filled wi orra folk
whaes stock-in-trade's the scrievit word,
or twicet-scrievit joke.
Brains, weak or strang, in heavy beer,
or ordinary, soak.
Quo yin: This yill is aafie dear,
I hae nae clinks in poke,
        nor fauldan-money,
in Embro to the ploy.

The auld Assembly-rooms, whaur Scott
forgethert wi his fiers,
nou see a gey kenspeckle lot
ablow the chandeliers.
Til Embro drouths the Festival Club
a richt godsend appears;
it's something new to find a pub
that gaes on sairvan beers
                eftir hours
in Embro to the ploy.

---

splore: frolic   *scrievit*: written   *clinks*: money   *poke*: pouch
fier: companion   *kenspeckle*: familiar   *ablow*: below

Jist pitten-out, the drucken mobs
frae howffs in Potterraw,
fleean, to hob-nob wi the Nobs,
ran to this Music Haa,
Register Rachel, Cougait Kate,
Nae-neb Nellie and aa
stauchert about amang the Great,
what fun! I never saw
    the like,
in Embro to the ploy.

They toddle hame doun lit-up streets
filled wi synthetic joy;
aweill, the year brings few sic treats
and muckle to annoy.
There's monie hartsom braw high-jinks
mixed up in this alloy
in simmer, whan aa sorts foregether
in Embro to the ploy.

stauchert: staggered

[b. 1936]

Choral Symphony

The customary conversation
Gives way to applause
For the Orchestra. Then
A roar, as Karajan
Takes the stand. He raises
His baton; the strings sweep in.

During the interval, we remain
Seated. Two Edinburgh ladies
Behind us complain:
'Such Teutonic discipline
Breeds perfection,
Not Art.' Their companion agrees.

At the end they join in,
As the ovation goes on
And on. What has changed their tune?
We overhear: 'Weren't the Chorus
Superb!' 'As one voice.'
'And that lace, on Muriel's dress.'

ROBERT GARIOCH
[1909–82]

Cooling-Aff

Het air is escaping frae St Andrew's Hous.
I'm on the Calton Hill. Level wi ma heid,
their lum is causing a wamble in the air,
nae reik, just a kinna shougle;
it's no the air ye see,
but a movement of something invisible.
Seen throu this movement, the Hume Toure
is liquid-like, a black flame.

It's nocht bit het air escaping;
the Government Offices are stecht wi'd,
pressurised, see whit a stishy,
yairds and yairds abuin the stack.
It's fair aafie inbye:
typewriters het to the touch,
fountain-pens wi safety-valves
to blaw aff steam frae the bilan ink,
their tea's owre het; they cannae drink it;
they cool it aff wi electric fans.

I'm even warm here masel
On the Calton Hill, Fowreteenth September,
Seiventy-twa, a fine back-end,
forbye the heat frae St Andrew's Hous.

Michtie. Nou it's cheengin direction;
it's coming strecht fir me,
And my pen has nae safety-valve.

lum: chimney	*wamble*: wobble	*reik*: smoke
shougle: shake	*stecht*: stuffed	*stishy*: violent motion

I rin to the tither side of the hill,
richt round the Temple of the Fowre Winds.

There's a gey cauld haar here,
snoovan up frae Leith Docks.

snoovan: moving quietly and smoothly

ROBERT GARIOCH
[1909–82]

A Wee Local Scandal

The University has got a wee
skyscraper at the corner of George Square,
fowerteen storeys, the day I wes there;
it's maybe sunk; I've no been back to see –

the Hume Toure – it hits ye in the ee,
yon muckle black rectangle in the air,
a graund sicht frae the Meedies, man; it fair
obliterates Arthur's Seat, nae word of a lee.

But whit a scandal. That's the Dauvit Hume
plewed in the professorial election;
hou can the outwail'd candidate presume

to name sic architectural perfection?
Dauvit Hume Toure, indeed. Whit a let-doun.
It shuid hae been the Will Cleghorn Erection.

LEWIS SPENCE
[1874–1955]

Craigentinnie

The fute fa's kind at Craigentinnie,
Saft is the gerss as emerald silk,
The air is sweet as Eprile milk
Or reamin' o' the heather hinny.

But the cauld whisper o' the sea
That haunted aince this marish place,
Tells o' the corpse-licht's eldritch race
On Craigentinnie lea.

And shipmen, smoor'd in tempests green
Lay stark and drooned alang the bog,
The deid-claith o' the dismal fog
Shrouding their cauld, wat een.

Snell is the wind upon the lea,
A grue frae aff a dreid despair,
The nicht brings dule, and bitter sair
The gurly whisper o' the sea.

ALAN BOLD

[b. 1943]

Edinburgh

In the street where people preen like princes
Edinburgh lays itself open like a secret solved:
The city juts into the sky, punctuates its space,
And the stone buildings bask in the light
That turns from blue to brilliant black.
Edinburgh is an experience,
A city of enormous gifts
Whose streets sing of history
Whose cobbles tell tales.
Philosophers strut in the squares,
The mob runs riot through the wynds,
Queen Mary and King Knox collide:
That's Edinburgh.
A city forms the folk conceived there
And we see the Edinburghers pass:
Pinstripe-suited legal types,
Wrecks rummaging in the Grassmarket,
Morningside ladies with their hats and patter,
Football fans heading for Easter Road,
Bits and pieces of humanity.
This city, green and gorgeous still,
Makes claims on its citizens.
There's no leaving Edinburgh,
No shifting it around:
It stays with you, always.
Always it stays with me.

NORMAN MACCAIG

[b. 1910]

Double Life

This wind from Fife has cruel fingers, scooping
The heat from streets with salty finger-tips
Crusted with frost; and all Midlothian,
Stubborn against what heeled the sides of ships
Off from the Isle of May, stiffens its drooping
Branches to the South. Each man
And woman put their winter masks on, set
In a stony flinch, and only children can
Light with a scream an autumn fire that says
With the quick crackle of its smoky blaze,
'Summer's to burn and it's October yet.'

My Water of Leith runs through a double city;
My city is threaded by a complex stream.
A matter of regret. If these cold stones
Could be stones only, and this watery gleam
Within the chasms of tenements and the pretty
Boskage of Dean could echo the groans
Of cart-wheeled bridges with only water's voice,
October would be just October. The bones
Of rattling winter would still lie underground,
Summer be less than ghost, I be unbound
From all the choking folderols of choice.

A loss of miracles – or an exchange
Of one sort for another. When the trams
Lower themselves like bugs on a branch down
The elbow of the Mound, they'd point the diagrams
Buckled between the New Town and the range
Of the craggy Old: that's all. A noun
Would so usurp all grammar no doing word
Could rob his money-bags or clap a crown
On his turned head, and all at last would be
Existence without category – free
From demonstration except as hill or bird.

And then no double-going stream would sing
Counties and books in the symbolic air,
Trundling my forty years to the Port of Leith.
But now, look around, my history's everywhere
And I'm my own environment. I cling
Like a cold limpet underneath
Each sinking stone and am the changing sea.
I die each dying moment and bequeath
Myself to all Octobers and to this
Damned flinty wind that with a scraping kiss
Howls that I'm winter, coming home to me.

[b. 1936]

Near Morebattle

'See that brown and white heifer on the far hill?
When the horizontal lines meet along the back and belly,
You fire. With a rifle like that you should hit
A stag in the neck at a quarter of a mile.
Even the Army'd find that hard to beat.' Out at three
In the morning he'd brought back the carcass of a deer
And the brush of a dog fox – knowing he was there
From a sudden rankness in the dewy air . . .

That night I take my new split-cane rod for a try-out
Upstream from where we are staying. Soon
It is too dark even to tie a bloodknot,
Or do more than sense in what pool I am casting.
On the way back I hear footsteps on iron.
Three men bar the bridge. 'Caught anything –?
The whitling should be up before long,
Worth waiting for that. What are you using,

Claret and grouse? Better with worm. See you then.'
They smile, and disappear. Able to hear
Only the water rippling on its stones, I picture
Both sides of a very different border
Where the snapping of twigs carries its own terror.
How lucky, that we can bring our children here,
To accessible streams untainted with fear,
And hills resplendent in their wearing of the green.

ROBERT LOUIS STEVENSON
[1850–94]

Blows the Wind Today

Blows the wind today and the sun and the rain are flying,
Blows the wind on the moor today and now,
Where about the graves of the martyrs the whaups are crying,
My heart remembers how.

Grey recumbent tombs of the dead in desert places,
Standing-stones on the vacant wine-red moor,
Hills of sheep and the homes of the silent vanquished races,
And winds austere and pure.

Be it granted me to behold you again in dying,
Hills of home! and to hear again the call,
Hear about the graves of the martyrs the peewees crying,
And hear no more at all.

[1850–94]

The Lamplighter

My tea is nearly ready, and the sun has left the sky;
It's time to take the window to see Leerie going by;
For every night at tea-time and before you take your seat,
With lantern and with ladder he comes posting up the street.

Now Tom would be a driver and Maria go to sea,
And my papa's a banker and as rich as he can be;
But I, when I am stronger and can choose what I'm to do,
O Leerie, I'll go round at night and light the lamps with you.

For we are very lucky, with a lamp before the door,
And Leerie stops to light it as he lights so many more;
And O! before you hurry by with ladder and with light,
O Leerie, see a little child and nod to him tonight.